Series consultant: Brian Williams
Author: Keith Lye
Educational consultant: Nigel Nelson

Illustrators: John Barber (pages 18–21, 28–31, 34–35, 44–45 & 58–71)
Jim Channell (pages 13, 50, 81, 86, 88, 90, 92, 94, 96 & 118–119)
Peter Goodfellow (pages 12–15, 22–25, 32–33, 38–43,
74–80, 100–114 & 118–119)
Kevin Maddison (silhouettes)
Larry Rostant (pages 48–49)
John Spires (pages 116–117)
Swanston Graphics (maps)
Ann Winterbotham (pages 51–58 & 61)
Paul Young (pages 26–27)
Cover art: James Goodridge & Andrew Hutchinson

Designer: Caroline Johnson
Editor: Camilla Hallinan

First American edition, 1993

YOUNG WORLD is a trademark of Random House, Inc.

Library of Congress Cataloging in Publication Data
Lye, Keith.
  Our planet earth / by Keith Lye.
  —1st American ed.
    p. cm.—(Young world; 5)
Includes index.
  Summary: Introduces the geology, geography,
climates, and natural resources of our planet.
  1. Earth—Juvenile literature. [1. Earth.]
I. Title. II. Series: Young world (New York, N.Y.)
QB631.4.L94   1993
550—dc20   92–21675

ISBN 0–679–83696–9
ISBN 0–679–93696–3 (lib.bdg.)

Manufactured in Spain
1 2 3 4 5 6 7 8 9 10

YOUNG WORLD

Our Planet
Earth

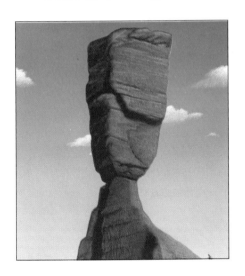

Random House New York

About YOUNG WORLD

For every young child, the world is full of new discoveries, new knowledge. It is important to have information books that enable even the youngest children to enjoy making these discoveries and gathering this knowledge for themselves.

YOUNG WORLD introduces a wide range of the topics that absorb children. The books in this series are all carefully prepared by specialist authors with the help of experienced educational advisers and teachers so that information is presented simply and memorably. Each book is complete in itself, yet builds into a multi-volume set – a real encyclopedia for the vital first years at school.

Because YOUNG WORLD books are small and easy to handle, children can dip into them on their own or read them with the help of a parent or a teacher. On each eye-catching page, a great deal of thought has been put into matching the clear, readable text with beautiful illustrations. These books are designed to encourage children to find facts for themselves, opening the door to a world where learning is fun.

Brian Williams, series consultant

About this book

Our planet, Earth, is amazing. With millions of
people and plants and animals, Earth is the only
place in the universe where we know for sure that life
exists. Our planet is very old, but it is always
changing. Earthquakes shake the land, and
volcanoes hurl blazing hot rock into the air.
Mountains are slowly pushed up and slowly worn
down again. Some places are dry and hot. Others
are covered in ice and snow.

Why is Earth so varied? And why is it always
changing? Turn the pages of this book and you will
find the answers to many questions like these. You
will find out how people use Earth and how they
change it. By learning about Earth, you can find out
how to look after it, too.

Keith Lye, author

CONTENTS

OUR PLANET

LAND

WATER

AROUND THE WORLD

PEOPLE AND EARTH

Our Earth

🌍 What is Earth?

Our planet Earth is a huge,
rocky ball. It is one of
the nine planets that
travel around
the sun.

If you were in
space, and you
could see
Earth, it would
look like this.

Earth looks blue
because most of it
is covered in water.
In fact, oceans, seas, and
lakes cover about seven-
tenths of our planet's surface.

The swirling patterns are white clouds. They are part of a thin layer of air around Earth.

This layer of air is called the atmosphere.

As far as we know, Earth is the only planet that has air we can breathe.

🌐 All kinds of places

Earth is a beautiful place with lots of different scenery. Some places are hot. Other places are cold and covered by ice and snow. In some parts, the land rises in high mountains and volcanoes.

Most people live in flat regions called plains. Grass covers some plains. Forest covers other areas.

People have changed the land. They have cut down forests and dug up grasslands to make farms. They have also built towns and cities and roads.

Amazing facts

🌍 Earth is not a perfect sphere, like a ball. It is slightly flat at the top, around the North Pole, and at the bottom, around the South Pole. It also bulges slightly in the middle, near the equator.

🌍 If you flew once around Earth you would travel about 24,800 miles.

🌍 Our planet Earth seems big, but it is really only a tiny part of the universe. The universe is made up of millions and millions of stars.

🌍 Earth is the only planet we know where living things can exist. But somewhere in the universe there might be another planet where there is life.

🌍 Earth is a rocky planet, like Mercury, Venus, Mars, and Pluto. The other planets – Jupiter, Saturn, Uranus and Neptune – are huge balls of gas.

Land

⛰ Under your feet

The outside of Earth is a thin shell of
hard rock with soil and water on top.
This shell is called the crust.

Soil is made of tiny pieces of ground-up
rock mixed with dead plants.

Plants get their water and some food
from the soil, through their roots.

Many animals live underground and
make their homes in the soil.

19

⛰ Rocks

Wherever you are on Earth, on land or sea, there is rock under you. There are three main types of rock.

Sedimentary rock is made when layers of things such as sand and seashells pile up. Eventually the bottom layers get squashed together to make rock. Limestone, chalk, and sandstone are sedimentary rocks.

shelly limestone

sandstone

chalk

Granite is a type of igneous rock.

Igneous rock is made when hot, melted rock from inside Earth rises, cools down, and hardens.

granite

Rock can be changed by being heated or squashed again. This type of rock is called metamorphic rock.

marble

Marble and slate are metamorphic rocks.

slate

▲▲ Record in rock

Many rocks form in layers, like a pile of sandwiches. You can see these layers in deep valleys or on cliff faces.

We can get an idea of the age of a layer of rock by studying the types of fossils in it.

1,700 million years old

550 million years old

250 million years old

Fossils are the hardened remains of dead plants and animals. Millions of years ago, animals called ammonites lived in the sea. When they died, their shells were covered with mud and layers of rock. The shapes of their shells are found in rocks as fossils.

Journey to the center

Earth is divided into three main parts:
the crust, the mantle, and the core.

1. The hard, rocky crust is about
25 miles thick under the land,
but only about 4 miles thick
under the sea.

2. The mantle is about 1,800
miles thick. It is hot, and
in some parts the rock
is melted. Melted or liquid
rock is called molten rock.

3. The core is even
hotter. It is about
2,600 miles thick.
The outer core is
made of liquid metal.
The inner core is the
hottest part. It is
made of solid metal.

⛰ Earthquakes

Earth's hard outer shell is divided into huge pieces called plates. The plates move very slowly. They are moved by currents in the molten rock underneath.

When the edges of two plates move suddenly, the ground shakes. We call this an earthquake. Earthquakes can make the land tremble so much that buildings fall down.

⏶ Volcanoes

A volcano is an opening in Earth's crust where molten rock can flow out. Molten rock is called magma when it is under the ground, and lava when it is on the surface.

When lava cools, it gets hard, and new rock is formed. Every time a volcano erupts, its lava makes another layer of rock. This is how some mountains are formed.

lava

vent

magma

▲▲ Mountains

It takes millions of years for big mountain ranges to be formed.

Many mountains are formed when two plates push against each other. The rocks on the edges of the plates are squeezed together and pushed up into big folds.

Some mountains are still rising. They have jagged peaks. Older mountains have rounded peaks because they have been worn down.

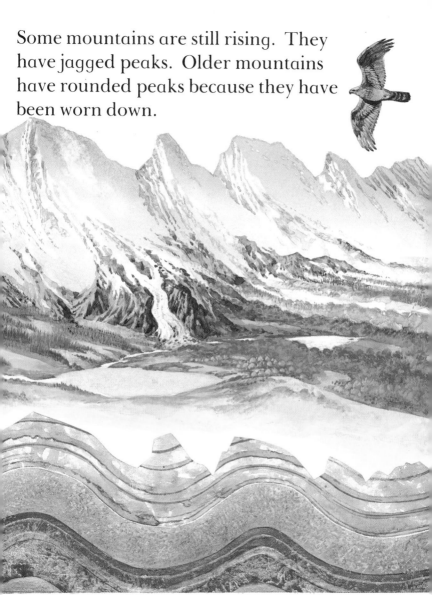

▲▲ Shaping the land

Things in nature are always wearing down the land. Winds blow sand up off the ground. The sand rubs away the rock like sandpaper. So the rock changes shape, very slowly, over many thousands of years.

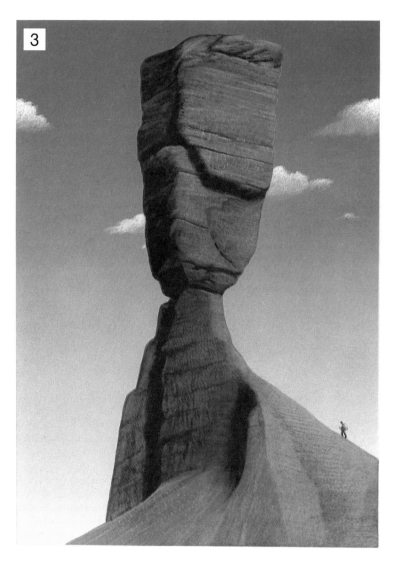

3

▲▲ Inside a cave

Water wears down the land. Ocean waves crash against the cliffs. Rainwater carves out pits, tunnels, and caves in limestone rock.

Sometimes rivers flow underground through the dark caves.

Minerals in the water dripping from the roof of this cave make stalagmites and stalactites. Stalagmites grow up from the floor; stalactites grow down from the roof. They grow less than ¼ inch each year.

Amazing facts

▲▲ Earth was formed about 4½ billion years ago. At first, its surface was probably covered by hot, molten rock. This cooled and hardened into a crust.

▲▲ The oldest known fossils are about 3½ billion years old. From later fossils we know that dinosaurs lived on Earth 200 million years ago and then disappeared about 65 million years ago.

▲▲ The world's highest mountain is Mount Everest, in the Himalayas. It stands on the border between two countries, Nepal and China, in Asia. It is 29,028 feet high.

▲▲ When stone is worn away by wind and rain, we call it weathering. You can see weathering in towns and cities, on old buildings, statues, and gravestones.

Water

◖ The sea

Most of Earth is covered with water.
Many animals live in the seas and oceans.
Fishermen catch some of these for us to eat.

coast   oil rig   fishing boats

trench

The oceans contain many other things
that are useful to us. Engineers pump
oil and gas from rock under the oceans.

Many volcanoes rise from the ocean floor. Some grow so high that they stick out of the water and form new islands. Some icebergs are as big as islands. They are pieces of ice that have broken away from a frozen coast.

island   iceberg

Under the oceans there are mountains, valleys, and plains. The deepest parts of the oceans are called trenches.

🌢 The water cycle

Water is carried from the sea
to the land and back again,
in the water cycle.

1. The sun heats the oceans.
The heat turns some sea water
into an invisible gas in the air.
This gas is called water vapor.

2. As the air rises and cools, the water
vapor turns into tiny drops of water.

3. The drops of water form clouds. Winds blow the clouds over the land.

4. Water in the clouds falls to the ground as rain, snow, or hail. The water runs over the land and soaks into the soil.

5. Rivers take some of the water to the sea. The water cycle starts again.

The life of a river

Rivers and streams carry water downhill to
the sea. A river usually grows wider and
flows more slowly as it gets nearer the sea.

Imagine the river as a
person, getting older
as it flows from
the mountains
to the sea.

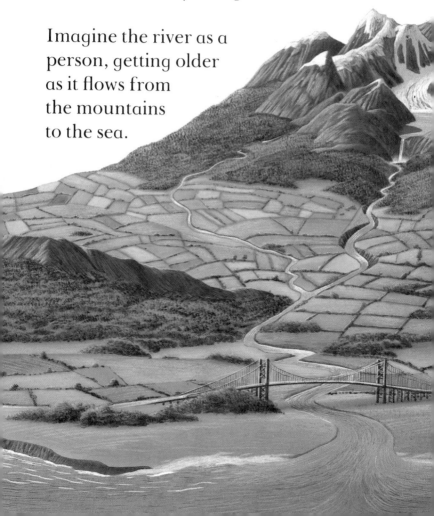

1. The young river

Some rivers start at the end of glaciers, where the ice melts. Some rivers flow out of lakes or from springs of water in the ground.

A river starting in the mountains falls steeply and flows quickly. It tumbles down over waterfalls and wears away deep valleys.

2. The middle-aged river

When the river leaves the mountains, it flows in bends called meanders.

3. The old river

Near the sea, the river flows slowly across an almost flat plain. It flows into the sea at its mouth.

Lakes and waterfalls

Lakes form in large hollows in the land.
Rivers flow in and out of most lakes.
Rivers bring mud and sand from other
places, so some lakes clog up and disappear.

Most waterfalls are found high up in the
mountains. They often form where rivers
flow over steep cliffs made of hard rock
that is not worn away easily.

Amazing facts

◊ There are four oceans: the Pacific, the Atlantic, the Indian, and the Arctic. The biggest is the Pacific Ocean. It is bigger than all the world's land areas put together.

◊ The deepest point in all the oceans is in the Marianas Trench in the Pacific Ocean. It is about 7 miles deep.

◊ The world's longest river is the Nile, in Africa. It is 4,144 miles long.

◊ Where magma heats underground water, hot water comes out of the ground. A kind of hot spring called a geyser can shoot out jets of water that are 100 feet high or more.

◊ Angel Falls in Venezuela, in South America, is 3,211 feet high. It is the world's tallest waterfall.

Air

🌥 What is air?

We cannot see it, taste it, or smell it, but air is all around us. Air is a mixture of invisible gases, mainly nitrogen and oxygen. People, animals, and plants need these gases to live. So if there was no air, there would be no life on Earth.

The air around Earth is called the atmosphere. It covers the whole planet like a blanket. It traps the heat from the sun to keep Earth warm. But it also protects us from the sun's harmful rays. Air is what brings different weather – hot and cold, wet and dry, windy and calm.

Higher up in the atmosphere, the air has less oxygen and nitrogen, and it gets colder. The air gradually gets thinner and thinner, until it ends and space begins.

☁ The wind

When air moves we call it wind.

Heat from the
sun warms the air
and makes it rise.

Cold air moves in
under the warm
air, and a wind
starts to blow.

Birds use warm
air to glide
through the sky.
They hardly flap
their wings,
because the warm
air carries them
up.

Wind speeds are measured on the Beaufort
scale.

Number 1 on the Beaufort scale is almost calm air. Number 4 is a breeze (about 15 miles per hour).

Number 7 is a moderate gale (about 35 miles per hour). Number 9 is a strong gale (about 60 miles per hour).

☁ Storms

Thunderstorms bring wind and rain.
Fiercer storms, called hurricanes,
sometimes form over the oceans.
When they reach land, hurricanes cause
enormous damage.

Tornadoes are whirlwinds that form over
land. As they spin along, they rip up trees
and buildings.

☁ Lightning and thunder

Electricity builds up inside big, dark storm clouds. The lightning we see is a giant spark of this electricity.

Lightning often travels from a cloud right down to the ground. Lightning is dangerous because of its huge electrical power.

Seconds later, we hear thunder crashing. Thunder is caused by lightning. When lightning heats up the air, waves of air push outward. This movement makes the rumbling sound we hear.

We hear thunder after we see the lightning because sound travels more slowly than light through the air.

☁ Clouds

Clouds are made of millions of tiny water droplets or ice crystals in the air. There are several kinds of clouds.

Clouds help people to forecast what sort of weather is on the way.

cumulus   cumulonimbus

cirrus

The highest clouds,
where the air is cold, are
made of ice crystals. They
are called cirrus clouds.

The largest clouds are
called cumulonimbus or
thunderclouds. They
bring heavy rain and hail.

stratus

Rain

Raindrops form when the tiny droplets of water in clouds join together. When the drops become big and heavy, they fall to the ground.

Plants need water to grow. So rain is very important for growing crops for food. Without enough rain, crops may die and there may not be enough food for people and animals.

Rice is a plant that needs lots of water. Farmers grow rice in fields called paddies that have low walls to hold in the rainwater.

In very cold air, water droplets freeze around ice crystals and fall as hailstones.

Snow and ice

In cold places, water freezes into ice,
and snow covers the land and the trees.
A snowflake is made of many tiny ice
crystals that have become stuck together.

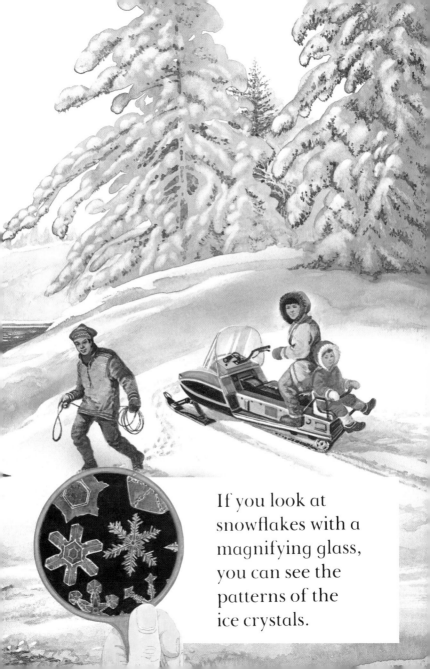

If you look at
snowflakes with a
magnifying glass,
you can see the
patterns of the
ice crystals.

☁ Cold lands

The usual weather in a place is called its climate. Climate affects the land. Antarctica, around the South Pole, has a very cold climate, so it is covered in ice.

The Arctic, around the North Pole, is also covered in ice and snow. But in summer some of the snow melts, in regions called tundra. Plants grow, and herds of caribou come to graze. Insects hatch out, and birds fly in to nest.

Forests and woods

Huge forests of evergreen trees (which don't lose their leaves in winter) grow in the northern parts of the world, where winters are long and cold.

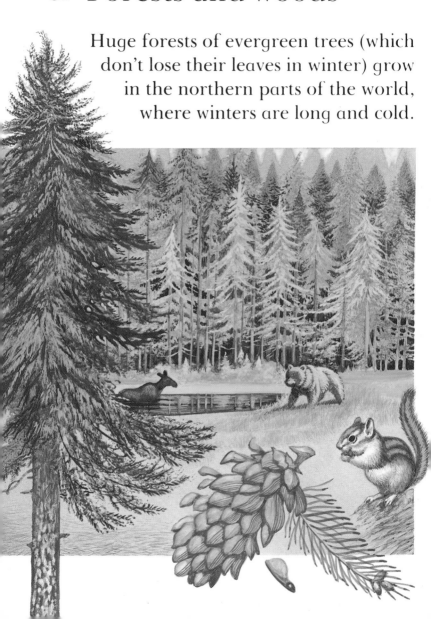

Other forests grow in countries with milder climates. Many trees in these forests are deciduous – they lose their leaves in winter.

The forests provide homes and food for many animals.

☁ Grasslands

In places with long dry seasons it is mainly grass that grows. There are very few trees.

Australia's grassland is called the bush. Kangaroos feed on the grass there.

Many animals live on the African grasslands, which are called savannas.

☁ Hot and dry

Deserts cover large parts of the world.
They get very little rain, so they have few
plants and animals – just a lot of sand and
rock. Wind blows the sand into huge hills
called dunes.

In some deserts, plant seeds lie in the
ground for years. The seeds come to life
only when there is a rainstorm.

Cactus plants in American deserts have thick, swollen stems that store water. They can live for months without any rain.

The jerboa is an animal that lives in the desert. It digs burrows underground and comes out to feed at night, when it is cool.

Rain forests

Rain forests grow in countries that are hot and have a lot of rain. More than half of the world's plant and animal species, or kinds, live in these forests.

The rain forests are in danger because people are cutting them down and turning them into farmland.

Amazing facts

☁ The world's driest place is the Atacama Desert in Chile, South America. One part has had no rain for 400 years.

☁ Mount Waialeale in Hawaii has more rainy days than anywhere else. It rains there about 350 days every year.

☁ Hailstones as big as tennis balls have fallen from the sky. In 1986, some hailstones weighing just over 2 pounds were reported in Bangladesh, in Asia.

☁ Antarctica is the coldest place on Earth. The world's lowest air temperature, minus 128.6 degrees Fahrenheit, was recorded there in 1983.

☁ The world's highest air temperature, 136.4 degrees Fahrenheit, was recorded in the Sahara desert in Libya, Africa, in 1922.

Earth

in space

Earth, sun, and moon

Earth is one of nine planets traveling around the sun. It takes a year to go around the sun. The sun is over 100 times the size of Earth.

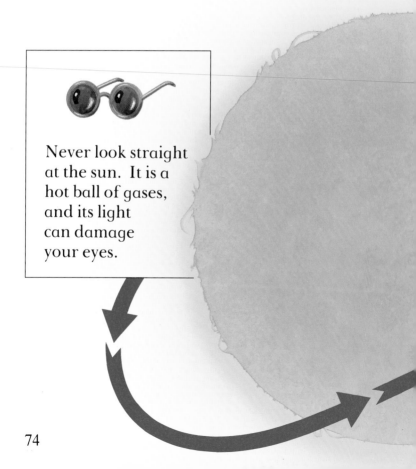

Never look straight at the sun. It is a hot ball of gases, and its light can damage your eyes.

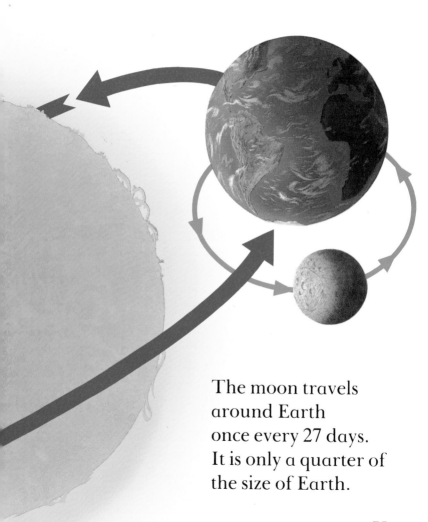

The moon travels
around Earth
once every 27 days.
It is only a quarter of
the size of Earth.

☜ Day and night

As well as traveling around the sun, Earth is spinning on its axis.

The axis is an imaginary line from the North Pole through the center of Earth to the South Pole.

Earth takes a day (24 hours) to make one complete turn on its axis.

South Pole

S

The part of Earth which faces the sun gets sunlight. As Earth spins around on its axis, that part turns away from the sun and becomes dark. This is why we have day and night in every 24 hours.

North Pole

Paris, nighttime

Paris, daytime

Long days, short days

Earth's axis is tilted by about 23½ degrees. So, as Earth travels around the sun, first one half (or hemisphere) of Earth leans toward the sun, then the other.

This is why the weather changes during the year, in the different seasons: summer, autumn, winter, and spring.

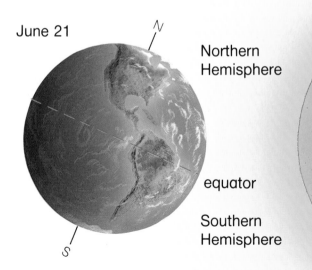

June 21

Northern Hemisphere

equator

Southern Hemisphere

The equator is an imaginary line that divides Earth into the two hemispheres.

June 21 is the first day of summer in the north because the Northern Hemisphere is leaning toward the sun. But it is the first day of winter in the Southern Hemisphere.

December 21 is the beginning of summer in the south, when the Southern Hemisphere leans toward the sun. But it is the first day of winter in the Northern Hemisphere.

December 21

So the seasons in the south are the opposite of those in the north.

79

☙ The seasons

In spring, days are warm and nights cool.
Summer days are hot and nights are warm.

In autumn, the days become cooler.
In winter, days and nights are cold.

Not everywhere has four seasons. The North and South Poles have two seasons, light and dark. During summer, the sun never sets. But in winter it does not rise.

In some places near the equator, there are two seasons: a dry season and a wet one.

Amazing facts

✦ One year on the calendar is 365 days. But Earth takes 365 days, 5 hours, and 46 seconds to complete one journey around the sun. To allow for this extra time, we add an extra day to the calendar every fourth year and call it a leap year.

✦ The moon was formed about the same time as Earth. We know this because scientists have worked out that the oldest rocks brought back by astronauts are about 4½ billion years old.

✦ There is no life on the moon, because it has no air or water.

✦ At Yuma, Arizona, the sun shines for more than 4,000 hours each year. This is about 11 hours every day.

✦ At the South Pole, the sun does not shine at all for 182 days each year.

Around

the world

Land and sea

Spread out on a flat map, the world looks like this. The compass points show which way is north, south, east, and west.

compass points

84

Earth has seven continents: Asia, Africa, North America, South America, Antarctica, Europe, and Australia.

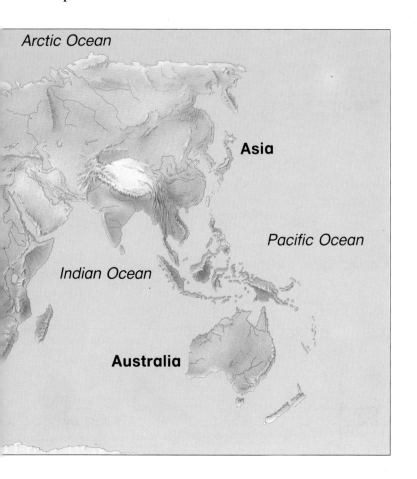

🌐 North America

Each continent is full of natural wonders. These are some of North America's interesting places:

Niagara Falls

The Rocky Mountains

Monument Valley, a rocky desert

An island in the Caribbean Sea

The numbers on the map show you where the places are.

🌐 South America

The Amazon River and the vast Amazon rain forest

The Andes, the world's longest chain of mountains

The Atacama Desert, the driest place in the world

Argentinian grasslands, called pampas

N

W ←⊙→ E

S

89

🌐 Europe

A Norwegian fjord, a valley carved out by glaciers

The Matterhorn in the Alps, a young mountain range

The Rhine River, which flows from the Alps to the sea

Coastline on the warm Mediterranean Sea

91

Asia

Mount Everest,
the world's highest
mountain

Oil wells in the
Arabian Desert

Rice fields in Japan,
a chain of volcanic
islands

N
W ←⊙→ E
S

93

Africa

The Sahara, the world's largest desert

The Nile, the longest river in the world

Mount Kilimanjaro, soaring above the savanna

Victoria Falls, on the wide Zambezi River

A volcanic island in the Pacific Ocean

Ayers Rock, in the center of Australia

The Murray River, the longest river in Australia

A geyser in New Zealand

Oceania is the name of a region that includes the continent of Australia, New Zealand, and many Pacific Ocean islands.

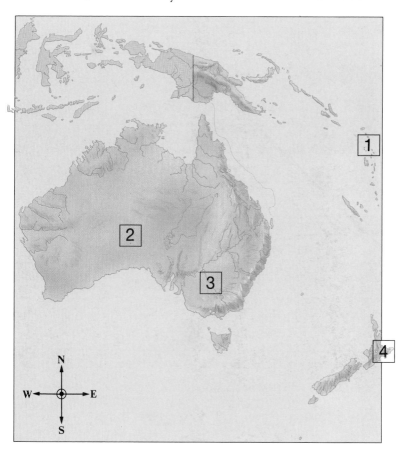

Amazing facts

🌐 Some scientists believe that all the continents were joined together until about 200 million years ago. If you look at the map of the world on pages 84–85, the shapes of the continents seem to match each other like the pieces of a giant jigsaw puzzle.

🌐 Australia is the only country that is also a continent. It is also the smallest continent.

🌐 The biggest continent is Asia. Asia is nearly six times as big as Australia.

🌐 The world has more than 5 billion people.

🌐 China, in Asia, has more than 1 billion people. No other country has as many people.

People and

Earth

▓▓ A changing landscape

People change Earth. They often turn land that was once forest into farmland.

When people cut down forest, plants and animals that lived there die out.

Farming families often live in villages. Other people come to the village to take their children to school, do their shopping, go to the post office, or see the doctor.

Villages often grow into towns. People build new houses on the farmland.

▄▄ Living in a city

About 200 years ago, most people lived on farms or in farming villages. But in many countries now, most people live in towns and cities.

Cities have big hospitals, schools, and stores. Cities also have factories and offices where people can work.

People travel around the busy streets by car or bus or train. Airplanes bring people from other cities far away.

Getting around

In some places, animals pull loads.

But cars are the main form of transportation for most people.

Trucks carry goods from place to place.

Ships carry heavy loads
across the oceans.

Trains carry freight
and passengers.

Airplanes carry people
around the
world.

⬛ Food from the land

Earth provides us with many resources. Resources are the things we need. Land is a resource. All over the world, farmers use the land to grow food for people.

The most important foods are grains, including corn, rice, and wheat.

cocoa

fruit

vegetables

tea

sugar

coffee

harvesting
wheat

corn

rice

wheat

oats

107

🏭 Animals on the land

As well as growing food crops, farmers keep animals on the land.

Cows provide milk. Some of their milk is used to make butter and cheese.

Chickens lay eggs.

Many people eat the meat of farm animals.

Sheep's wool is used to make clothes.

🏭 Fish from the sea

Another important food is fish. Many kinds of fish swim in the seas around the world.

Fishermen use nets to catch fish. Their boats bring the fish back to land.

■ Timber from the forest

Forests provide timber for building houses and making furniture. Even the paper in this book is made from wood.

Rubber trees provide sap for making rubber. Tires and gloves are some of the things made from rubber.

wood

rubber

When trees are cut down, new trees must be planted.

⬛ Earth's riches

The rocks in Earth's crust contain many valuable things, such as the fuels we need.

Coal is used as fuel. Miners dig it out of the ground. Some coal mines are very deep.

Two other important fuels are oil and gas. They are found in the ground and under the sea bed.

Miners on a rig drill holes into the rock. Then the oil or the gas is pumped up.

🏭 Our garbage

When factories and power stations burn fuel, they pump smoke and gases into the air. This pollutes the air. So do exhaust fumes from traffic.

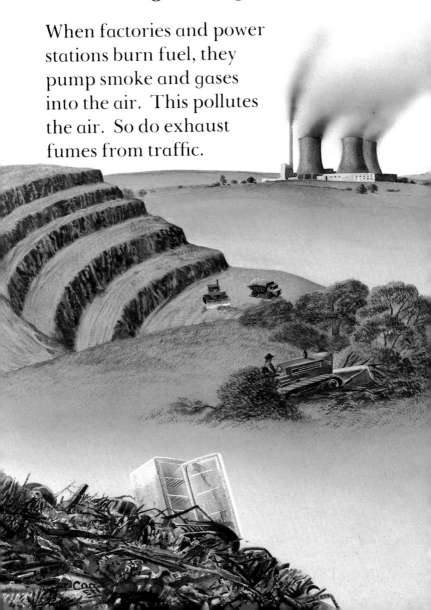

Towns and factories pump sewage and poisonous chemicals into rivers and seas. This pollutes the water and harms the plants and animals living in it.

Farmers spray their crops with chemicals that harm the soil. And people litter the countryside with garbage.

![factory icon] Looking after Earth

Everyone can help to make Earth a clean and healthy place for all living things.

We can help to keep Earth beautiful by planting trees.

Trees provide food and homes for many animals. They also help to keep the air clean.

We can help to keep Earth clean by being careful about our garbage.

A lot of our garbage can be recycled. Recycling means making new things from old materials.

bottle banks

These pieces of garbage can be recycled.

glass

metal

paper

rubber

plastic

old clothes

If we recycle our empty glass bottles, they can be melted down to make new glass.

Using things again is less wasteful. So recycling helps to save Earth's resources.

🏭 Our planet

Since the start of the space age,
we have been able to see
what our planet looks like.

Spacecraft take
photographs that
show us Earth's
continents and its
white clouds and
blue oceans.

Earth is our home.
If we harm Earth
and waste its resources,
we have nowhere else to go.

No other planet has air and water and all the other things we need.

So we must all look after our beautiful home, Earth.

119

Amazing facts

Every year around the world, people are cutting down an area of rain forest roughly equal to the size of Greece.

Some scientists think that 50 kinds of plants and animals become extinct every day because their homes in the rain forests are being destroyed. Extinct plants and animals are gone forever.

In 1991, Mexico City was the world's largest city. Over 20 million people live there. That means it has more people than the continent of Australia.

Recycling one ton of waste paper can save 15 trees from being cut down to make new paper.

INDEX